POCKET-SIZED

THEME PARK VACATION PLANNER

Weekend Edition

CONTENTS

TRIP INFORMATION

Dates: _____

_____

_____

Transportation: _____

_____

_____

_____

_____

_____

Lodging: _____

_____

_____

_____

_____

_____

Other: _____

_____

_____

_____

_____

_____

_____

(i)

VACATION AT A GLANCE

Day 1:	Day 2:

Day 3:	Day 4:

DAY 1

Date:_____

Reminders:

Dining:_____
_____
_____
_____
_____

Plan:_____
_____
_____
_____
_____
_____
_____
_____
_____
_____

DAY 2

Date:_____

Reminders:

Dining:_____

_____
_____
_____
_____
_____

Plan:_____

_____
_____
_____
_____
_____
_____
_____
_____
_____
_____

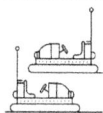

DAY 3

Date: _____

Reminders:

Dining: _____
_____
_____
_____
_____

Plan: _____
_____
_____
_____
_____
_____
_____
_____
_____

DAY 4

Date:_____

Reminders:

Dining:_____

_____

_____

_____

_____

Plan:_____

_____

_____

_____

_____

_____

_____

_____

_____

EXPENSE TRACKER

Date	Description	Type	Amount

Dining(D), Lodging (L), Other (O), Souvenirs (S), Transportation (T)

Date	Description	Type	Amount

Dining(D), Lodging (L), Other (O), Souvenirs (S), Transportation (T)

Date	Description	Type	Amount

Dining(D), Lodging (L), Other (O), Souvenirs (S), Transportation (T)

Date	Description	Type	Amount

Dining(D), Lodging (L), Other (O), Souvenirs (S), Transportation (T)

PRE-TRIP PLANNING

Deadline	Task	Done

Deadline	Task	Done

Deadline	Task	Done

Deadline	Task	Done

RIDES & EXPERIENCES WISH LIST

✓	Ride/Experience	Park/Location	Notes

DINING WISH LIST

✓	Restaurant	Park/Location	Notes

PACKING LIST

NOTES

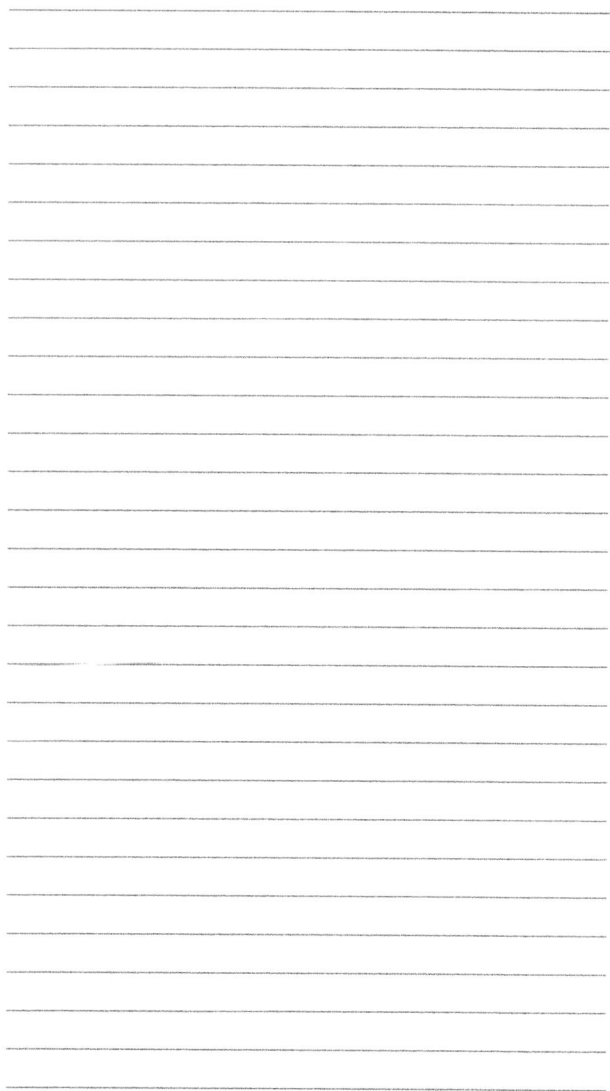

PUBLISHER'S NOTE

Thank you for choosing this planner!

If you like this planner, please help others find it by leaving a review online where you purchased it.

You can learn more about the author of this planner, and her other books, by visiting heidikinney.com.

Have a wonderful vacation!

www.ingramcontent.com/pod-product-compliance
Lightning Source LLC
Chambersburg PA
CBHW071803020426
42331CB00008B/2388